FOUR AMERICANS

FOUR AMERICANS

ROOSEVELT
HAWTHORNE
EMERSON
WHITMAN

BY

HENRY A. BEERS

AUTHOR OF

STUDIES IN AMERICAN LITERATURE
A HISTORY OF ENGLISH ROMANTICISM

Essay Index Reprint Series

Originally published by:

YALE UNIVERSITY PRESS

97231

BOOKS FOR LIBRARIES PRESS
FREEPORT, NEW YORK

First Published 1919
Reprinted 1968

Reprinted from a copy in the collections of
The New York Public Library
Astor, Lenox and Tilden Foundations

LIBRARY OF CONGRESS CATALOG CARD NUMBER:

68-54324

MANUFACTURED
BY
HALLMARK LITHOGRAPHERS, INC.
IN THE U.S.A.

CONTENTS

ROOSEVELT AS MAN OF LETTERS

IN a club corner, just after Roosevelt's
death, the question was asked whether his
memory would not fade away, when the living
man, with his vivid personality, had gone.
But no: that personality had stamped itself
too deeply on the mind of his generation to
be forgotten. Too many observers have recorded their impressions; and already a
dozen biographies and memoirs have ap-
peared. Besides, he is his own recorder. He
published twenty-six books, a catalogue of
which any professional author might be
proud; and a really wonderful feat when it
is remembered that he wrote them in the
intervals of an active public career as Civil
Service Commissioner, Police Commissioner,
member of his state legislature, Governor of
New York, delegate to the National Republican Convention, Colonel of Rough Riders,
Assistant Secretary of the Navy, Vice-
President and President of the United
States.

Perhaps in some distant future he may
become a myth or symbol, like other mighty
hunters of the beast, Nimrod and Orion and
Tristram of Lyonesse. Yet not so long as

"African Game Trails" and the "Hunting Trips of a Ranchman" endure, to lift the imagination to those noble sports denied to the run of mortals by poverty, feebleness, timidity, the engrossments of the humdrum, everyday life, or lack of enterprise and opportunity. Old scraps of hunting song thrill us with the great adventure: "In the wild chamois' track at break of day"; "We'll chase the antelope over the plain"; "Afar in the desert I love to ride"; and then we go out and shoot at a woodchuck, with an old double-barrelled shotgun—and miss! If Roosevelt ever becomes a poet, it is while he is among the wild creatures and wild landscapes that he loved: in the gigantic forests of Brazil, or the almost unnatural nature of the Rockies and the huge cattle ranches of the plains, or on the limitless South African veldt, which is said to give a greater feeling of infinity than the ocean even.

Roosevelt was so active a person—not to say so noisy and conspicuous; he so occupied the centre of every stage, that, when he died, it was as though a wind had fallen, a light had gone out, a military band had stopped playing. It was not so much the death of an individual as a general lowering in the vitality of the nation. America was less America, because he was no longer here. He should have lived twenty years more had he

been willing to go slow, to loaf and invite his
soul, to feed that mind of his in a wise pas-
siveness. But there was no repose about
him, and his pleasures were as strenuous as
his toils. John Burroughs tells us that he
did not care for fishing, the contemplative
man's recreation. No contemplation for
him, but action; no angling in a clear stream
for a trout or grayling; but the glorious,
dangerous excitement of killing big game—
grizzlies, lions, African buffaloes, mountain
sheep, rhinoceroses, elephants. He never
spared himself: he wore himself out. But
doubtless he would have chosen the crowded
hour of glorious life—or strife, for life and
strife were with him the same.

He was above all things a fighter, and the
favorite objects of his denunciation were
professional pacifists, nice little men who had
let their muscles get soft, and nations that
had lost their fighting edge. Aggressive war,
he tells us in "The Winning of the West," is
not always bad. "Americans need to keep
in mind the fact that, as a nation, they have
erred far more often in not being willing
enough to fight than in being too willing."
"Cowardice," he writes elsewhere, "in a race,
as in an individual, is the unpardonable sin."
Is this true? Cowardice is a weakness, perhaps a disgraceful weakness: a defect of
character which makes a man contemptible,

just as foolishness does. But it is not a sin at all, and surely not an unpardonable one. Cruelty, treachery, and ingratitude are much worse traits, and selfishness is as bad. I have known very good men who were cowards; men that I liked and trusted but who, from weakness of nerves or other physical causes—perhaps from prenatal influences— were easily frightened and always constitutionally timid. The Colonel was a very pugnacious man: he professed himself to be a lover of peace—and so did the Kaiser— but really he enjoyed the *gaudium certaminis*, as all bold spirits do.

In the world-wide sense of loss which followed his death, some rather exaggerated estimates made themselves heard. A preacher announced that there had been only two great Americans, one of whom was Theodore Roosevelt. An editor declared that the three greatest Americans were Washington, Lincoln, and Roosevelt. But not all great Americans have been in public life; and, of those who have, very few have been Presidents of the United States. What is greatness? Roosevelt himself rightly insists on character as the root of the matter. Still character alone does not make a man great. There are thousands of men in common life, of sound and forceful character, who never become great, who are not

even potentially great. To make them such,
great abilities are needed, as well as favor-
ing circumstances. In his absolute manner—a manner caught perhaps partly from
Macaulay, for whose qualities as a writer he
had a high and, I think, well-justified regard—he pronounces Cromwell the greatest
Englishman of the seventeenth century.
Was he so? He was the greatest English
soldier and magistrate of that century; but
how about Bacon and Newton, about
Shakespeare and Milton?

Let us think of a few other Americans
who, in their various fields, might perhaps
deserve to be entitled great. Shall we say
Jonathan Edwards, Benjamin Franklin,
Alexander Hamilton, John Marshall, Robert
Fulton, S. F. B. Morse, Ralph Waldo Emerson, Daniel Webster, Horace Greeley, Henry
Ward Beecher, Admiral Farragut, General
W. T. Sherman, James Russell Lowell,
Nathaniel Hawthorne, General Robert E.
Lee? None of these people were Presidents
of the United States. But to the man in
the street there is something imposing about
the office and title of a chief magistrate, be
he emperor, king, or elected head of a republic. It sets him apart. Look at the crowds
that swarm to get a glimpse of the President
when he passes through, no matter whether
it is George Washington or Franklin Pierce.

It might be safer, on the whole, to say
that the three names in question are those
of our greatest presidents, not of the greatest Americans. And even this comparison
might be questioned. Some, for example,
might assert the claims of Thomas Jefferson
to rank with the others. Jefferson was a
man of ideas who made a strong impression
on his generation. He composed the Decla-
ration of Independence and founded the
Democratic party and the University of
Virginia. He had a more flexible mind than
Washington, though not such good judg-
ment; and he had something of Roosevelt's
alert interest in a wide and diversified range
of subjects. But the latter had little patience with Jefferson. He may have re-
spected him as the best rider and pistol shot
in Virginia; but in politics he thought him
a theorist and doctrinaire imbued with the
abstract notions of the French philosophical
deists and democrats. Jefferson, he thought,
knew nothing and cared nothing about military affairs. He let the army run down and
preferred to buy Louisiana rather than con-
quer it, while he dreamed of universal frater-
nity and was the forerunner of the Dove of
Peace and the League of Nations.

Roosevelt, in fact, had no use for philosophy or speculative thought which could
not be reduced to useful action. He was an

eminently practical thinker. His mind was
without subtlety, and he had little imagination. A life of thought for its own sake;
the life of a dreamer or idealist; a life like
that of Coleridge, with his paralysis of will
and abnormal activity of the speculative
faculty, eternally spinning metaphysical cob-
webs, doubtless seemed to the author of
"The Strenuous Life" a career of mere self-
indulgence. It is not without significance
that, with all his passion for out of doors,
for wild life and the study of bird and beast,
he nowhere, so far as I can remember, men-
tions Thoreau,* who is far and away our
greatest nature writer. Doubtless he may
have esteemed him as a naturalist, but not
as a transcendentalist or as an impracti-
cable faddist who refused to pay taxes because Massachusetts enforced the fugitive
slave law. We are told that his fellow historian, Francis Parkman, had a contempt
for philosophers like Emerson and Thoreau
and an admiration for writers such as Scott
and Cooper who depicted scenes of bold adventure. The author of "The Oregon
Trail" and the author of "African Game
Trails" had a good deal in common, espe-

* Mr. Edwin Carty Ranck, of the Roosevelt Memo-
rial Committee, calls attention to the following sentence, which I had overlooked: "As a woodland
writer, Thoreau comes second only to Burroughs."—
"The Wilderness Hunter," p. 261.

cially great force of will—you see it in
Parkman's jaw. He was a physical wreck
and did his work under almost impossible
conditions; while Roosevelt had built up an
originally sickly constitution into a physique
of splendid vigor.

Towards the critical intellect, as towards
the speculative, Roosevelt felt an instinctive
antagonism. One of his most characteristic
utterances is the address delivered at the
Sorbonne, April 30, 1910, "Citizenship in a
Republic." Here, amidst a good deal of
moral commonplace—wise and sensible for
the most part, but sufficiently platitudi-
nous—occurs a burst of angry eloquence.
For he was always at his strongest when
scolding somebody. His audience included
the intellectual *élite* of France; and he warns
it against the besetting sin of university dons
and the learned and lettered class in general,
a supercilious, patronizing attitude towards
the men of action who are doing the rough
work of the world. Critics are the object of
his fiercest denunciation. "A cynical habit
of thought and speech, a readiness to criticise
work which the critic himself never tries to
perform, an intellectual aloofness which will
not accept contact with life's realities—all
these are marks, not, as the possessor would
fain think, of superiority, but of weakness. . . . It is not the critic who counts;

14

not the man who points out how the strong
man stumbles, or where the doer of deeds
could have done them better. . . . Shame on
the man of cultivated taste who permits refinement to develop into a fastidiousness that
unfits him for doing the rough work of a
workaday world. Among the free peoples
who govern themselves there is but a small
field of usefulness open for the men of
cloistered life who shrink from contact with
their fellows."

The speaker had seemingly himself been
stung by criticism; or he was reacting
against Matthew Arnold, the celebrated
"Harvard indifference," and the cynical talk
of the clubs.

We do not expect our Presidents to be
literary men and are correspondingly grati-
fied when any of them shows signs of almost
human intelligence in spheres outside of
politics. Of them all, none touched life at
so many points, or was so versatile, picturesque, and generally interesting a figure as
the one who has just passed away. Washington was not a man of books. A country
gentleman, a Virginia planter and slave-
owner, member of a landed aristocracy, he
had the limited education of his class and
period. Rumor said that he did not write
his own messages. And there is a story that
John Quincy Adams, regarding a portrait

15

of the father of his country, exclaimed, "To think that that old wooden head will go down in history as a great man!" But this was the comment of a Boston Brahmin, and all the Adamses had bitter tongues. Washington was, of course, a very great man, though not by virtue of any intellectual brilliancy, but of his strong character, his immense practical sagacity and common sense, his leadership of men.

As to Lincoln, we know through what cold obstruction he struggled up into the light, educating himself to be one of the soundest statesmen and most effective public speakers of his day—or any day. There was an in-born fineness or sensitiveness in Lincoln, a touch of the artist (he even wrote verses) which contrasts with the phlegm of his illustrious contemporary, General Grant. The latter had a vein of coarseness, of com-monness rather, in his nature; evidenced by his choice of associates and his entire indif-ference to "the things of the mind." He was almost illiterate and only just a gentleman. Yet by reason of his dignified modesty and simplicity, he contrived to write one of the best of autobiographies.

Roosevelt had many advantages over his eminent predecessors. Of old Knickerbocker stock, with a Harvard education, and the habit of good society, he had means enough to indulge in his favorite pastimes. To run a cattle ranch in Dakota, lead a hunting party in Africa and an exploring expedition in Brazil, these were wide opportunities, but he fully measured up to them. Mr. W. H. Hays, chairman of the Republican National Committee, said of him, "He had more knowledge about more things than any other man." Well, not quite that. We have all known people who made a specialty of omniscience. If a man can speak two languages besides his own and can read two more fairly well, he is at once credited with knowing half a dozen foreign tongues as well as he knows English. Let us agree, however, that Roosevelt knew a lot about a lot of things. He was a rapid and omnivorous reader, reading a book with his finger tips, gutting it of its contents, as he did the birds that he shot, stuffed, and mounted; yet not inappreciative of form, and accustomed to recommend much good literature to his countrymen. He took an eager interest in a large variety of subjects, from Celtic poetry and the fauna and flora of many regions to simplified spelling and the split infinitive.

A young friend of mine was bringing out, for the use of schools and colleges, a volume of selections from the English poets, all learnedly annotated, and sent me his manuscript to look over. On a passage about the bittern bird he had made this note, "The bittern has a harsh, throaty cry." Whereupon I addressed him thus: "Throaty nothing! You are guessing, man. If Teddy Roosevelt reads your book—and he reads everything—he will denounce you as a nature faker and put you down for membership in the Ananias Club. Recall what he did to Ernest Seton-Thompson and to that minister in Stamford, Connecticut. Remember how he crossed swords with Mr. Scully touching the alleged dangerous nature of the ostrich and the early domestication of the peacock. So far as I know, the bittern thing has no voice at all. His real stunt is as follows. He puts his beak down into the swamp, in search of insects and snails or other marine life—*est-ce que je sais?*—and drawing in the bog-water through holes in his beak, makes a booming sound which is most impressive. Now do not think me an ornithologist or a bird sharp. Personally I do not know a bittern from an olive-backed thrush. But I have read some poetry, and I remember what Thomson says in 'The Seasons':

> The bittern knows his time with bill ingulf'd
> To shake the sounding marsh.

See also 'The Lady of the Lake':

> And the bittern sound his drum,
> Booming from the sedgy shallow.

See even old Chaucer who knew a thing or two about birds, *teste* his 'Parlament of Foules,' admirably but strangely edited by Lounsbury, whose indifference to art was only surpassed by his hostility to nature. Says Chaucer:

And as a bytoure bumblith in the myre."

My friend canceled his note. It is, of course, now established that the bittern "booms"—not in the mud—but in the air.

Mr. Roosevelt was historian, biographer, essayist, and writer of narrative papers on hunting, outdoor life, and natural history, and in all these departments did solid, important work. His "Winning of the West" is little, if at all, inferior in historical interest to the similar writings of Parkman and John Fiske. His "History of the Naval War of 1812" is an astonishing performance for a young man of twenty-four, only two years out of college. For it required a careful sifting of evidence and weighing of authorities. The job was done with patient thoroughness, and the book is accepted, I believe, as authoritative. It is to me a somewhat tedious tale. One sea fight is much like another, a record of meaningless slaughter. Of the three lives, those of Gouverneur Morris, T. H. Benton, and Oliver Cromwell, I cannot speak with confidence, having read only the last. I should guess that the life of Benton was written more *con amore* than the others, for the frontier was this historian's favorite scene. The life of Cromwell is not so much a formal biography as a continuous essay in interpretation of a character still partly enigmatic in spite of all the light that so many acute psychologists have shed upon it. It is a relief to read for once a book which is without preface, footnote, or reference. It cannot be said that the biographer contributes anything very new to our knowledge of his subject. The most novel features of his work are the analogies that he draws between situations in English and American political history. These are usually ingenious and illuminating, sometimes a little misleading; as where he praises Lincoln's readiness to acquiesce in the result of the election in 1864 and to retire peaceably in favor of McClellan; contrasting it with Cromwell's dissolution of his Parliaments and usurpation of the supreme power. There was a certain likeness in the exigencies, to be sure, but a broad difference between the problems confronting the two rulers. Lincoln was a constitutional President with strictly limited powers, bound by usage and precedent. For him to have kept his seat by military force, in defiance of a Democratic majority, would have been an act of treason.

But the Lord Protector held a new office, unknown to the old constitution of England and with ill-defined powers. A revolution had tossed him to the top and made him dictator. He was bound to keep the peace in unsettled times, to keep out the Stuarts, to keep down the unruly factions. If Parliament would not help, he must govern without it. Carlyle thought that he had no choice.

Roosevelt's addresses, essays, editorials, and miscellaneous papers, which fill many volumes, are seldom literary in subject, and certainly not in manner. He was an effective speaker and writer, using plain, direct, forcible English, without any graces of style. In these papers he is always the moralist, earnest, high-minded, and the preacher of many gospels: the gospel of the strenuous life; the gospel of what used to be called "muscular Christianity"; the gospel of large families; of hundred per cent Americanism; and, above all, of military preparedness. I am not here concerned with the President's political principles, nor with the specific measures that he advocated. I will only say, to guard against suspicion of unfair prejudice, that, as a Democrat, a free-trader, a state-rights man, individualist, and anti-imperialist, I naturally disapproved of many acts of his administration, of the administration of his predecessor, and of his party in general. I disapproved, and still do, of the McKinley and Payne-Aldrich tariffs; of the Spanish war—most avoidable of wars—with its sequel, the conquest of the Philippines; above all, of the seizure of the Panama Canal zone.

But let all that pass: I am supposed to be dealing with my subject as man of letters. As such the Colonel of the Rough Riders was the high commander-in-chief of rough writers. He never persuaded his readers into an opinion—he bullied them into it. When he gnashed his big teeth and shook his big stick,

> . . . The bold Ascalonite
> Fled from his iron ramp; old warriors turned
> Their plated backs under his heel;

mollycoddles, pussy-footers, professional pacifists, and nice little men who had lost their fighting edge, all scuttled to cover. He called names, he used great violence of language. For instance, a certain president of a woman's college had "fatuously announced . . . that it was better to have one child brought up in the best way than several not thus brought up." The woman making this statement, wrote the Colonel, "is not only unfit to be at the head of a female college, but is not fit to teach the lowest class in a kindergarten; for such teaching is not merely folly, but a peculiarly repulsive type

of mean and selfish wickedness." And again:
"The man or woman who deliberately avoids
marriage . . . is in effect a criminal against
the race and should be an object of con-
temptuous abhorrence by all healthy people."

Now, I am not myself an advocate of race
suicide but I confess to a feeling of sympathy
with the lady thus denounced, whose point of
view is, at least, comprehensible. Old Mal-
thus was not such an ass as some folks think.
It is impossible not to admire Roosevelt's
courage, honesty, and wonderful energy:
impossible to keep from liking the man for
his boyish impulsiveness, camaraderie, sport-
ing blood, and hatred of a rascal. But it is
equally impossible for a man of any spirit
to keep from resenting his bullying ways, his
intolerance of quiet, peaceable people and
persons of an opposite temperament to his
own. Even nice, timid little men who have
let their bodies get soft do not like to be
bullied. It puts their backs up. His ideal
of character was manliness, a sound ideal,
but he insisted too much upon the physical
side of it, "red-bloodedness" and all that.
Those poor old fat generals in Washington
who had been enjoying themselves at their
clubs, playing bridge and drinking Scotch
highballs! He made them all turn out and
ride fifty miles a day.

Mr. Roosevelt produced much excellent

23

literature, but no masterpieces like Lincoln's Gettysburg Address and Second Inaugural. Probably his sketches of ranch life and of hunting trips in three continents will be read longest and will keep their freshness after the public questions which he discussed have lost interest and his historical works have been in part rewritten. In these outdoor papers, besides the thrilling adventures which they—very modestly—record, there are even passages of descriptive beauty and chapters of graphic narrative, like the tale of the pursuit and capture of the three robbers who stole the boats on the Missouri River, which belonged to the Roosevelt ranch. This last would be a capital addition to school readers and books of selected standard prose.

Senator Lodge and other friends emphasize the President's sense of humor. He had it, of course. He took pains to establish the true reading of that famous retort, "All I want out of you is common civility and damned little of that." He used to repeat with glee Lounsbury's witticism about "the infinite capability of the human mind to resist the introduction of knowledge." I wonder whether he knew of that other good saying of Lounsbury's about the historian Freeman's being, in his own person, a proof of the necessity of the Norman Conquest.

He had, at all events, a just and high estimate of the merits of my brilliant colleague. "Heu quanto minus est cum reliquis versari quam tui meminisse!" But Roosevelt was not himself a humorist, and his writings give little evidence of his possession of the faculty. Lincoln, now, was one of the foremost American humorists. But Roosevelt was too strenuous for the practice of humor, which implies a certain relaxation of mind: a detachment from the object of immediate pursuit: a superiority to practical interests which indulges itself in the play of thought; and, in the peculiarly American form of it, a humility which inclines one to laugh at himself. Impossible to fancy T. R. making the answer that Lincoln made to an applicant for office: "I haven't much influence with this administration." As for that variety of humor that is called irony, it demands a duplicity which the straight-out-speaking Roosevelt could not practise. He was like Epaminondas in the Latin prose composition book, who was such a lover of truth that he never told a falsehood even in jest—*ne joco quidem.*

The only instance of his irony that I recall—there may be others—is the one recorded by Mr. Leupp in his reply to Senator Gorman, who had charged that the examiners of the Civil Service Commission had turned down "a bright young man" in the city of Baltimore, an applicant for the position of letter-carrier, "because he could not tell the most direct route from Baltimore to Japan." Hereupon the young Civil Service Commissioner challenged the senator to verify his statement, but Mr. Gorman preserved a dignified silence. Then the Commissioner overwhelmed him in a public letter from which Mr. Leupp quotes the closing passage, beginning thus: "High-minded, sensitive Mr. Gorman! Clinging, trustful Mr. Gorman! Nothing could shake his belief in that 'bright young man.' Apparently he did not even yet try to find out his name—if he had a name," and so on for nearly a page. Excellent fooling, but a bit too long and heavy-handed for the truest ironic effect.

Many of our Presidents, however little given to the use of the pen, have been successful coiners of phrases—phrases that have stuck: "entangling alliances," "era of good feeling," "innocuous desuetude," "a condition, not a theory." Lincoln was happiest at this art, and there is no need to mention any of the scores of pungent sayings which he added to the language and which are in daily use. President Roosevelt was no whit behind in this regard. All recognize and remember the many phrases to which he gave birth or currency: "predatory wealth," "bull moose," "hit the line hard," "weasel words," "my hat is in the ring," and so on. He took a humorous delight in mystifying the public with recondite allusions, sending everyone to the dictionary to look out "Byzantine logothete," and to the Bible and cyclopedia to find Armageddon.

Roosevelt is alleged to have had a larger personal following than any other man lately in public life. What a testimony to his popularity is the "teddy bear"; and what a sign of the universal interest, hostile or friendly, which he excited in his contemporaries, is the fact that Mr. Albert Shaw was able to compile a caricature life of him presenting many hundred pictures! There was something German about Roosevelt's standards. In this last war he stood heart and soul for America and her allies against Germany's misconduct. But he admired the Germans' efficiency, their highly organized society, their subordination of the individual to the state. He wanted to Prussianize this great peaceful republic by introducing universal obligatory military service. He insisted, like the Germans, upon the *Hausfrau's* duty to bear and rear many children. If he had been a German, it seems possible that, with his views as to the right of strong races to expand, by force if necessary, he might have justified the seizure of Silesia, the partition of Poland, the *Drang nach Osten*, and maybe even the invasion of Belgium—as a military measure.

And so of religion and the church, which Germans regard as a department of government. Our American statesman, of course, was firmly in favor of the separation of church and state and of universal toleration. But he advises everyone to join the church, some church, any old church; not because one shares its beliefs—creeds are increasingly unimportant—but because the church is an instrument of social welfare, and a man can do more good in combination with his fellows than when he stands alone. There is much truth in this doctrine, though it has a certain naïveté, when looked at from the standpoint of the private soul and its spiritual needs.

As in the church, so in the state, he stood for the associative principle as opposed to an extreme individualism. He was a practical politician and therefore an honest partisan, feeling that he could work more efficiently for good government within party lines than outside them. He resigned from the Free Trade League because his party was committed to the policy of protection. In 1884 he supported his party's platform and candidate, instead of joining the Mugwumps and voting for Cleveland, though at the National Republican Convention, to which he went as a delegate, he had opposed the nomination of Blaine. I do not believe that his motive in this decision was selfish, or that he quailed under the snap of the party lash because he was threatened with political death in case he disobeyed. Theodore Roosevelt was nobody's man. He thought, as he frankly explained, that one who leaves his faction for every slight occasion, loses his influence and his power for good. Better to compromise, to swallow some differences and to stick to the crowd which, upon the whole and in the long run, embodies one's convictions. This is a comprehensible attitude, and possibly it is the correct one for the man in public life who is frequently a candidate for office. Yet I wish he could have broken with his party and voted for Cleveland. For, ironically enough, it was Roosevelt himself who afterward split his party and brought in Wilson and the Democrats.

Disregarding his political side and considering him simply as man of letters, one seeks for comparisons with other men of letters who were at once big sportsmen and big writers; Christopher North, for example: "Christopher in his Aviary" and "Christopher in his Shooting Jacket." The likeness here is only a very partial one, to be sure.

The American was like the Scotchman in his athleticism, high spirits, breezy optimism, love of the open air, intense enjoyment of life. But he had not North's roystering conviviality and uproarious Toryism; and the kinds of literature that they cultivated were quite unlike.

Charles Kingsley offers a closer resemblance, though the differences here are as numerous as the analogies. Roosevelt was not a clergyman, and not a creative writer, a novelist, or poet. His temperament was not very similar to Kingsley's. Yet the two shared a love for bold adventure, a passion for sport, and an eager interest in the life of animals and plants. Sport with Kingsley took the shape of trout fishing and of riding to hounds, not of killing lions with the rifle. He was fond of horses and dogs; associated democratically with gamekeepers, grooms, whippers-in, poachers even; as Roosevelt did with cowboys, tarpon fishers, wilderness guides, beaters, trappers, and all whom Walt Whitman calls "powerful uneducated persons," loving them for their pluck, coolness, strength, and skill. Kingsley's "At Last, a Christmas in the West Indies," exhibits the same curiosity as to tropical botany and zoölogy that Roosevelt shows in his African and Brazilian journeys. Not only tastes, but many ideals and opinions the two men had in common. "Parson Lot," the Chartist and Christian Socialist, had the same sympathy with the poor and the same desire to improve the condition of agricultural laborers and London artisans which led Roosevelt to promote employers' liability laws and other legislation to protect the workingman from exploitation by conscienceless wealth. Kingsley, like Roosevelt, was essentially Protestant. Neither he nor Mr. Roosevelt liked asceticism or celibacy. As a historian, Kingsley did not rank at all with the author of "The Winning of the West" and the "Naval War of 1812." On the other hand, if Roosevelt had written novels and poetry, I think he would have rejoiced greatly to write "Westward Ho," "The Last Buccaneer," and "Ode to the North-East Wind."

In fine, whatever lasting fortune may be in store for Roosevelt's writings, the disappearance of his vivid figure leaves a blank in the contemporary scene. And those who were against him can join with those who were for him in slightly paraphrasing Carlyle's words of dismissal to Walter Scott, "Theodore Roosevelt, pride of all Americans, take our proud and sad farewell."

FIFTY YEARS OF HAWTHORNE

HAWTHORNE was an excellent critic of his own writings. He recognizes repeatedly the impersonal and purely objective nature of his fiction. R. H. Hutton once called him the ghost of New England; and those who love his exquisite, though shadowy, art are impelled to give corporeal substance to this disembodied spirit: to draw him nearer out of his chill aloofness, by associating him with people and places with which they too have associations.

I heard Colonel Higginson say, in a lecture at Concord, that if a few drops of redder blood could have been added to Hawthorne's style, he would have been the foremost imaginative writer of his century. The ghosts in "The Æneid" were unable to speak aloud until they had drunk blood. Instinctively, then, one seeks to infuse more red corpuscles into the somewhat anæmic veins of these tales and romances. For Hawthorne's fiction is almost wholly ideal. He does not copy life like Thackeray, whose procedure is inductive: does not start with observed characters, but with an imagined problem or situation of the soul, inventing characters to fit. There is always a dreamy quality about the action: no violent quarrels, no passionate love scenes. Thus it has been often pointed out that in "The Scarlet Letter" we do not get the history of Dimmesdale's and Hester's sin: not the passion itself, but only its sequels in the conscience. So in "The House of the Seven Gables," and "The Marble Faun," a crime has preceded the opening of the story, which deals with the working out of the retribution.

When Hawthorne handled real persons, it was in the form of the character sketch— often the satirical character sketch,—as in the introduction to "The Scarlet Letter" which scandalized the people of Salem. If he could have made a novel out of his custom-house acquaintances, he might have given us something less immaterial. He felt the lack of solidity in his own creations: the folly of constructing "the semblance of a world out of airy matter"; the "value hidden in petty incidents and ordinary characters." "A better book than I shall ever write was there," he confesses, but "my brain wanted the insight and my hand the cunning to transcribe it."

Now and then, when he worked from observation, or utilized his own experiences, a piece of drastic realism results. The suicide of Zenobia is transferred, with the necessary changes, from a long passage in "The American Note Books," in which he tells of going out at night, with his neighbors, to drag for the body of a girl who had drowned herself in the Concord. Yet he did not refrain the touch of symbolism even here. There is a wound on Zenobia's breast, inflicted by the pole with which Hollingsworth is groping the river bottom.

And this is why one finds his "American Note Books" quite as interesting reading as his stories. Very remarkable things, these note books. They have puzzled Mr. James, who asks what the author would be at in them, and suggests that he is writing letters to himself, or practising his hand at description. They are not exactly a *journal intime;* nor are they records of thought, like Emerson's ten volumes of journals. They are carefully composed, and are full of hints for plots, scenes, situations, characters, to be later worked up. In the three collections, "Twice-Told Tales," "Mosses from an Old Manse," and "The Snow Image," there are, in round numbers, a hundred tales and sketches; and Mr. Conway has declared that, in the number of his original plots, no modern author, save Browning, has equalled Hawthorne. Now, the germ of many, if not most, of these inventions may be found in some brief jotting—a paragraph, or a line or two—in "The American Note Books."

Yet it is not as literary material that these notes engage me most—by far the greater portion were never used,—but as records of observation and studies of life. I will even acknowledge a certain excitement when the diarist's wanderings lead him into my own neighborhood, however insignificant the result. Thus, in a letter from New Haven in 1830, he writes, "I heard some of the students at Yale College conjecturing that I was an Englishman." Mr. Lathrop thinks that it was on this trip through Connecticut that he hit upon his story, "The Seven Vagabonds," the scene of which is near Stamford, in the van of a travelling showman, where the seven wanderers take shelter during a thunderstorm. How quaintly true to the old provincial life of back-country New England are these figures—a life that survives to-day in out-of-the-way places. Holgrave, the young daguerreotypist in "The House of the Seven Gables," a type of the universal Yankee, had practised a number of these queer trades: had been a strolling dentist, a lecturer on mesmerism, a salesman in a village store, a district schoolmaster, editor of a country newspaper; and "had subsequently travelled New England and the Middle States, as a peddler, in the employment of a Connecticut manufactory of Cologne water and other essences." The Note Books tell us that,

at North Adams in 1838, the author fore-
gathered with a surgeon-dentist, who was
also a preacher of the Baptist persuasion:
and that, on the stage-coach between Worcester and Northampton, they took up an
essence-vender who was peddling anise-seed,
cloves, red-cedar, wormwood, opodeldoc,
hair-oil, and Cologne water. Do you imagine
that the essence-peddler is extinct? No, you
may meet his covered wagon to-day on lonely
roads between the hill-villages of Massachusetts and Connecticut.

It was while living that strange life of
seclusion at Old Salem, compared with which
Thoreau's hermitage at Walden was like the
central roar of Broadway, that Hawthorne
broke away now and then from his solitude,
and went rambling off in search of contacts
with real life. Here is another item that he
fetched back from Connecticut under date
of September, 1838: "In Connecticut and
also sometimes in Berkshire, the villages are
situated on the most elevated ground that
can be found, so that they are visible for
miles around. Litchfield is a remarkable instance, occupying a high plain, without the
least shelter from the winds, and with almost
as wide an expanse of view as from a moun-
tain-top. The streets are very wide—two or
three hundred feet at least—with wide green
margins, and sometimes there is a wide green

space between two road tracks. . . . The
graveyard is on the slope, and at the foot
of a swell, filled with old and new grave-
stones, some of red freestone, some of gray
granite, most of them of white marble and
one of cast iron with an inscription of raised
letters." Do I not know that wind-swept
hilltop, those grassy avenues? Do I not
know that ancient graveyard, and what names
are on its headstones? Yes, even as the heart
knoweth its own bitterness.

As we go on in life, anniversaries become
rather melancholy affairs. The turn of the
year—the annual return of the day—birth-
days or death-days or set festal occasions
like Christmas or the New Year, bring re-
minders of loss and change. This is true of
domestic anniversaries; while public literary
celebrations, designed to recall to a forgetful
generation the centenary or other dates in
the lives of great writers, appear too often
but milestones on the road to oblivion. Fifty
years is too short a time to establish a literary immortality; and yet, if any American
writer has already won the position of a
classic, Hawthorne is that writer. Speaking
in this country in 1883, Matthew Arnold
said: "Hawthorne's literary talent is of the
first order. His subjects are generally not
to me subjects of the highest interest; but
his literary talent is . . . the finest, I think,

which America has yet produced—finer, by much, than Emerson's." But how does the case stand to-day? I believe that Hawthorne's fame is secure as a whole, in spite of the fact that much of his work has begun to feel the disintegrating force of hostile criticism, and "the unimaginable touch of time."

For one thing, American fiction, for the past fifty years, has been taking a direction quite the contrary of his. Run over the names that will readily occur of modern novelists and short-story writers, and ask yourself whether the vivid coloring of these realistic schools must not inevitably have blanched to a still whiter pallor those visionary tales of which the author long ago confessed that they had "the pale tints of flowers that blossomed in too retired a shade." With practice has gone theory; and now the critics of realism are beginning to nibble at the accepted estimates of Hawthorne. A very damaging bit of dissection is the recent essay by Mr. W. C. Brownell, one of the most acute and unsparingly analytic of American critics. It is full of cruelly clever things: for example, "Zenobia and Miriam linger in one's memory rather as brunettes than as women." And again, à propos of Roger Chillingworth in "The Scarlet Letter,"—"His characters are not creations, but expedients." I admire these sayings; but they seem to me, like most epigrams, brilliant statements of half-truths. In general, Mr. Brownell's thesis is that Hawthorne was spoiled by allegory: that he abused his naturally rare gift of imagination by declining to grapple with reality, which is the proper material for the imagination, but allowing his fancy—an inferior faculty— to play with dreams and symbols; and that consequently he has left but one masterpiece.

This is an old complaint. Long ago, Edgar Poe, who did not live to read "The Scarlet Letter," but who wrote a favorable review of "The Twice-Told Tales," advised the author to give up allegory. In 1880, Mr. Henry James wrote a life of Hawthorne for the English Men of Letters series. This was addressed chiefly to the English public and was thought in this country to be a trifle unsympathetic; in particular in its patronizing way of dwelling upon the thinness of the American social environment and the consequent provincialism of Hawthorne's books. The "American Note Books," in particular, seem to Mr. James a chronicle of small beer, and he marvels at the triviality of an existence which could reduce the diarist to recording an impression that "the aromatic odor of peat smoke in the sunny autumnal air is very pleasant." This peat-smoke entry has become proverbial, and is mentioned by nearly everyone who writes about Hawthorne. Yet on a recent re-reading of James's biography, it seemed to me not so unsympathetic as I had remembered it; but, in effect, cordially appreciative. He touches, however, on this same point, of the effect on Hawthorne's genius of his allegorizing habit. "Hawthorne," says Mr. James, "was not in the least a realist—he was not, to my mind, enough of one." The biographer allows him a liberal share of imagination, but adds that most of his short tales are more fanciful than imaginative. "Hawthorne, in his metaphysical moods, is nothing if not allegorical, and allegory, to my sense, is quite one of the lighter exercises of the imagination. Many excellent judges, I know, have a great stomach for it; they delight in symbols and correspondences, in seeing a story told as if it were another and a very different story. I frankly confess that it has never seemed to me a first-rate literary form. It is apt to spoil two good things—a story and a moral."

Except in that capital satire, "The Celestial Railroad," an ironical application of "The Pilgrim's Progress" to modern religion, Hawthorne seldom uses out-and-out allegory; but rather a more or less definite symbolism. Even in his full-length romances, this mental habit persists in the typical and, so to speak, algebraic nature of his figures and incidents. George Woodberry and others have drawn attention to the way in which his fancy clings to the physical image that represents the moral truth: the minister's black veil, emblem of the secret of every human heart; the print of a hand on the heroine's cheek in "The Birthmark," a sign of earthly imperfection which only death can eradicate; the mechanical butterfly in "The Artist of the Beautiful," for which the artist no longer cares, when once he has embodied his thought. Zenobia in "The Blithedale Romance" has every day a hot-house flower sent down from a Boston conservatory and wears it in her hair or the bosom of her gown, where it seems to express her exotic beauty. It is characteristic of the romancer that he does not specify whether this symbolic blossom was a gardenia, an orchid, a tuberose, a japonica, or what it was. Thoreau, if we can imagine him writing a romance, would have added the botanical name.

"Rappacini's Daughter" is a very representative instance of those "insubstantial fictions for the illustration of moral truths, not always of much moment." The suggestion of this tale we find in a quotation from Sir Thomas Browne in "The American Note Books" for 1837: "A story there passeth of an Indian King that sent unto Alexander a fair woman fed with aconite and other poisons, with this intent complexionally to destroy him." Here was one of those morbid situations, with a hint of psychological possibilities and moral applications, that never failed to fascinate Hawthorne. He let his imagination dwell upon it, and gradually evolved the story of a physician who made his own daughter the victim of a scientific experiment. In this tale, Mr. Brownell thinks, the narrative has no significance apart from the moral; and yet the moral is quite lost sight of in the development of the narrative, which might have been more attractive if told simply as a fairy tale. This is quite representative of Hawthorne's usual method. There is no explicit moral to "Rappacini's Daughter." But there are a number of parallels and applications open to the reader. He may make them, or he may abstain from making them as he chooses. Thus we are vaguely reminded of Mithridates, the Pontic King, who made himself immune to poisons by their daily employment. The doctor's theory, that every disease can be cured by the use of the appropriate poison, suggests the aconite and belladonna of the homeopathists and their motto, *similia similibus curantur*. Again we think of Holmes's novel "Elsie Venner," of the girl impregnated with the venom of the rattlesnake, whose life ended when the serpent nature died out of her; just as Beatrice, in Hawthorne's story, is killed by the powerful antidote which slays the poison. A very obvious incidental reflection is the cruelty of science, sacrificing its best loved object to its curiosity. And may we not turn the whole tale into a parable of the isolation produced by a peculiar and unnatural rearing, say in heterodox beliefs, or unconventional habits, unfitting the victim for society, making her to be shunned as dangerous?

The lure of the symbolic and the marvelous tempted Hawthorne constantly to the brink of the supernatural. But here his art is delicate. The old-fashioned ghost is too robust an apparition for modern credulity. The modern ghost is a "clot on the brain." Recall the ghosts in Henry James's "The Turn of the Screw"—just a suspicion of evil presences. The true interpretation of that story I have sometimes thought to be, that the woman who saw the phantoms was mad. Hawthorne is similarly ambiguous. His apparently preternatural phenomena always admit of a natural explanation. The water of Maule's well may have turned bitter in consequence of an ancient wrong; but also perhaps because of a disturbance in the underground springs. The sudden deaths of

Colonel and Judge Pyncheon may have been
due to the old wizard's curse that "God
would give them blood to drink"; or simply
to an inherited tendency to apoplexy. *Did*
Donatello have furry, leaf-shaped ears, or
was this merely his companions' teasing?
Did old Mistress Hibben, the sister of Governor Bellingham of Massachusetts, attend
witch meetings in the forest, and inscribe her
name in the Black Man's book? Hawthorne
does not say so, but only that the people so
believed; and it is historical fact that she
was executed as a witch. Was a red letter
A actually seen in the midnight sky, or was
it a freak of the aurora borealis? What did
Chillingworth see on Dimmesdale's breast?
The author will not tell us. But if it was
the mark of the Scarlet Letter, may we not
appeal to the phenomena of stigmatism: the
print, for example, of the five wounds of
Christ on the bodies of devotees? Hawthorne does not vouch for the truth of Alice
Pyncheon's clairvoyant trances: he relates
her story as a legend handed down in the
Pyncheon family, explicable, if you please,
on natural grounds—what was witchcraft in
the seventeenth century having become mesmerism or hypnotism in the nineteenth.

Fifty years after his death, Hawthorne is
already a classic. For even Mr. Brownell
allows him one masterpiece, and one master-

piece means an immortality. I suppose it is generally agreed that "The Scarlet Letter" is his *chef-d'œuvre*. Certainly it is his most intensely conceived work, the most thoroughly fused and logically developed; and is free from those elements of fantasy, mystery, and unreality which enter into his other romances. But its unrelieved gloom, and the author's unrelaxing grasp upon his theme, make it less characteristic than some of his inferior works; and I think he was right in preferring "The House of the Seven Gables," as more fully representing all sides of his genius. The difference between the two is the difference between tragedy and romance. While we are riding the high horse of criticism and feeling virtuous, we will concede the superiority of the former *genre;* but when we give our literary conscience the slip, we yield ourselves again to the fascination of the haunted twilight.

The antique gabled mansion in its quiet back street has the charm of the still-life sketches in the early books, such as "Sights from a Steeple," "A Rill from the Town Pump," "Sunday at Home," and "The Tollgatherer's Day." All manner of quaint figures, known to childhood, pass along that visionary street: the scissors grinder, town crier, baker's cart, lumbering stage-coach, charcoal vender, hand-organ man and monkey, a drove of cattle, a military parade—the "trainers," as we used to call them. Hawthorne had no love for his fellow citizens and took little part in the modern society of Salem. But he had struck deep roots into the soil of the old witch town, his birthplace and the home of generations of his ancestors. Does the reader know this ancient seaport, with its decayed shipping and mouldering wharves, its silted up harbor and idle customhouse, where Hawthorne served three years as surveyor of the port? Imposing still are the great houses around the square, built by retired merchants and shipmasters whose fortunes were made in the East India trade: with dark old drawing-rooms smelling of sandalwood and filled with cabinets of Oriental curiosities. Hawthorne had little to do with the aristocracy of Salem. But something of the life of these old families may be read in Mrs. Stoddard's novel "The Morgesons,"—a book which I am perpetually recommending to my friends, and they as perpetually refusing to read, returning my copy after a superficial perusal, with uncomplimentary comments upon my taste in fiction.

Hawthorne's academic connections are of particular interest. It is wonderful that he and Longfellow should have been classmates at Bowdoin. Equally wonderful that Emer-

son's "Nature" and Hawthorne's "Mosses"
should have been written in the same little
room in the Old Manse at Concord. It gives
one a sense of how small New England was
then, and in how narrow a runway genius
went. Bowdoin College in those days was a
little country school on the edge of the
Maine wilderness, only twenty years old, its
few buildings almost literally planted down
among the pine stumps. Hawthorne's
class—1825—graduated but thirty-seven
strong. And yet Hawthorne and Longfellow were not intimate in college but belonged to different sets. And twelve years
afterward, when Longfellow wrote a friendly
review of "Twice-Told Tales" in *The North
American Review*, his quondam classmate
addressed him in a somewhat formal letter
of thanks as "Dear Sir." Later the relations
of the two became closer, though never perhaps intimate. It was Hawthorne who
handed over to Longfellow that story of
the dispersion of the Acadian exiles of
Grandpré, which became "Evangeline": a
story which his friend Conolly had suggested
to Hawthorne, as mentioned in "The American Note Books." The point which arrested
Hawthorne's attention was the incident in
the Bayou Teche, where Gabriel's boat
passes in the night within a few feet of the

bank on which Evangeline and her company are sleeping.

This was one of those tricks of destiny that so often engaged Hawthorne's imagination: like the tale of "David Swan" the farmer's boy who, on his way to try his fortune in the city, falls asleep by a wayside spring. A rich and childless old couple stop to water their horse, are taken by his appearance and talk of adopting him, but drive away on hearing someone approaching. A young girl comes by and falls so much in love with his handsome face that she is tempted to waken him with a kiss, but she too is startled and goes on. Then a pair of tramps arrive and are about to murder him for his money, when they in turn are frightened off. Thus riches and love and death have passed him in his sleep; and he, all unconscious of the brush of the wings of fate, awakens and goes his way. Again, our romancer had read the common historical accounts of the great landslide which buried the inn in the Notch of the White Mountains. The names were known of all who had been there that night and had consequently perished—with one exception. One stranger had been present, who was never identified: Hawthorne's fancy played with this curious problem, and he made out of it his story of "The Ambitious Guest," a youth just starting on a brilliant career, entertaining the company around the fire, with excited descriptions of his hopes and plans; and then snuffed out utterly by ironic fate, and not even numbered among the missing.

Tales like these are among the most characteristic and original of the author's works. And wherever we notice this quality in a story, we call it Hawthornish. "Peter Rugg, the Missing Man," is Hawthornish; so is "Peter Schemil, the Man without a Shadow"; or Balzac's "Peau de Chagrin"; or later work, some of it manifestly inspired by Hawthorne, like Stevenson's tale of a double personality, "Dr. Jekyll and Mr. Hyde"; or Edward Bellamy's "Dr. Heidenhoff's Process"—a process for ensuring forgetfulness of unpleasant things—a modern water of Lethe. Even some of James's early stories like "The Madonna of the Future" and "The Last of the Valerii," as well as Mr. Howells's "Undiscovered Country," have touches of Hawthorne.

Emerson and Hawthorne were fellow townsmen for some years at Concord, and held each other in high regard. One was a philosophical idealist: the other, an artist of the ideal, who sometimes doubted whether the tree on the bank, or its image in the stream was the more real. But they took no impress from one another's minds. Emerson could not read his neighbor's romances. Their morbid absorption in the problem of evil repelled the resolute optimist. He thought the best thing Hawthorne ever wrote was his "Recollections of a Gifted Woman," the chapter in "Our Old Home" concerning Miss Delia Bacon, originator of the Baconian theory of Shakespeare, whom Hawthorne befriended with unfailing patience and courtesy during his Liverpool consulship.

Hawthorne paid a fine tribute to Emerson in the introduction to "Mosses from an Old Manse," and even paid him the honor of quotation, contrary to his almost invariable practice. I cannot recall a half dozen quotations in all his works. I think he must have been principled against them. But he said he had come too late to Concord to fall under Emerson's influence. No risk of that, had he come earlier. There was a jealous independence in Hawthorne which resented the too close approach of an alien mind: a species of perversity even, that set him in contradiction to his environment. He always fought shy of literary people. During his Liverpool consulship, he did not make—apparently did not care to make— acquaintance with his intellectual equals. He did not meet Carlyle, Dickens, Thackeray, Tennyson, Mill, Grote, Charles Reade, George Eliot, or any other first-class minds.

He barely met the Brownings, but did not
really come to know them till afterwards in
Italy. Surrounded by reformers, abolition-
ists, vegetarians, comeouters and radicals of
all gospels, he remained stubbornly conservative. He held office under three Democratic
administrations, and wrote a campaign life
of his old college friend Franklin Pierce when
he ran for President. Commenting on
Emerson's sentence that John Brown had
made the gallows sacred like the cross, Hawthorne said that Brown was a blood-stained
fanatic and justly hanged.

This conservatism was allied with a certain
fatalism, hopelessness, and moral indolence
in Hawthorne's nature. Hollingsworth, in
"The Blithedale Romance," is his picture of
the one-ideaed reformer, sacrificing all to his
hobby. Hollingsworth's hobby is prison
reform, and characteristically Hawthorne
gives us no details of his plan. It is vague-
ness itself, and its advocate is little better
than a type. Holgrave again, in "The
House of the Seven Gables," is the scornful
young radical; and both he and Hollingsworth are guilty of the mistake of supposing
that they can do anything directly to improve the condition of things. God will
bring about amendment in his own good
time. And this fatalism again is subtly
connected with New England's ancestral

creed—Calvinism. Hawthorne—it has been pointed out a hundred times—is the Puritan romancer. His tales are tales of the conscience: he is obsessed with the thought of sin, with the doctrines of foreordination and total depravity. In the theological library which he found stowed away in the garret of the Old Manse, he preferred the seventeenth-century folio volumes of Puritan divinity to the thin Unitarian sermons and controversial articles in the files of *The Christian Examiner*. The former, at least, had once been warm with a deep belief, however they had now "cooled down even to the freezing point." But "the frigidity of the modern productions" was "inherent." Hawthorne was never a church-goer and adhered to no particular form of creed. But speculatively he liked his religion thick.

> The Psalm-tunes of the Puritan,
>   The songs that dared to go
> Down searching through the abyss of man,
>   His deeps of conscious woe—

spoke more profoundly to his soul than the easy optimism of liberal Christianity. Hawthorne was no transcendentalist: he went to Brook Farm, not as a Fourierite or a believer in the principles of association, but attracted by the novelty of this experiment at communal living, and by the interesting

varieties of human nature there assembled:
literary material which he used in "The
Blithedale Romance." He complains slyly of
Miss Fuller's transcendental heifer which
hooked the other cows (though Colonel Higginson once assured me that this heifer was
only a symbol, and that Margaret never
really owned a heifer or cow of any kind).

Mr. Lathrop proposed, as a rough formula
for Hawthorne, Poe and Irving *plus* something of his own. The resemblances and differences between Poe and Hawthorne are
obvious. The latter never deals in physical
horror: his morbidest tragedy is of a spiritual kind; while once only—in the story entitled "William Wilson"—Poe enters that
field of ethical romance which Hawthorne
constantly occupies. What he has in common with Irving is chiefly the attitude of
spectatorship, and the careful refinement of
the style, so different from the loud, brassy
manner of modern writing. Hawthorne
never uses slang, dialect, oaths, or colloquial
idioms. The talk of his characters is book
talk. Why is it that many of us find this
old-fashioned elegance of Irving and Hawthorne irritating? Is it the fault of the
writer or of the reader? Partly of the
former, I think: that anxious finish, those
elaborately rounded periods have something
of the artificial, which modern naturalism

has taught us to distrust. But also, I believe, the fault is largely our own. We have grown so nervous, in these latter generations, so used to short cuts, that we are impatient of anything slow. Cut out the descriptions, cut out the reflections, *coupez vos phrases.* Hawthorne's style was the growth of reverie, solitude, leisure—"fine old leisure," whose disappearance from modern life George Eliot has lamented. On the walls of his study at the "Wayside" was written— though not by his own hand—the motto, "There is no joy but calm."

Sentiment and humor do not lie so near the surface in Hawthorne as in Irving. He had a deep sense of the ridiculous, well shown in such sketches as "P's Correspondence" and "The Celestial Railroad"; or in the description of the absurd old chickens in the Pyncheon yard, shrunk by in-breeding to a weazened race, but retaining all their top-knotted pride of lineage. Hawthorne's humor was less genial than Irving's, and had a sharp satiric edge. There is no merriment in it. Do you remember that scene at the Villa Borghese, where Miriam and Donatello break into a dance and all the people who are wandering in the gardens join with them? The author meant this to be a burst of wild mænad gaiety. As such I do not recall a more dismal failure. It is cold at the heart

of it. It has no mirth, but is like a dance
without music: like a dance of deaf mutes
that I witnessed once, pretending to keep
time to the inaudible scrapings of a deaf and
dumb fiddler.

Henry James says that Hawthorne's
stories are the only good American historical
fiction; and Woodberry says that his method
here is the same as Scott's. The truth of
this may be admitted up to a certain point.
Our Puritan romancer had certainly steeped
his imagination in the annals of colonial New
England, as Scott had done in his border
legends. He was familiar with the docu-
ments—especially with Mather's "Magnalia,"
that great source book of New England
poetry and romance. But it was not the
history itself that interested him, the broad
picture of an extinct society, the *tableau
large de la vie*, which Scott delighted to
paint; rather it was some adventure of the
private soul. For example, Lowell had told
him the tradition of the young hired man
who was chopping wood at the backdoor of
the Old Manse on the morning of the Concord fight; and who hurried to the battle-
field in the neighboring lane, to find both
armies gone and two British soldiers lying
on the ground, one dead, the other wounded.
As the wounded man raised himself on his
knees and stared up at the lad, the latter,

obeying a nervous impulse, struck him on the head with his axe and finished him. "The story," says Hawthorne, "comes home to me like truth. Oftentimes, as an intellectual and moral exercise, I have sought to follow that poor youth through his subsequent career and observe how his soul was tortured by the blood-stain. . . . This one circumstance has borne more fruit for me than all that history tells us of the fight." How different is this bit of pathology from the public feeling of Emerson's lines:

> Spirit that made those heroes dare
>   To die and leave their children free,
> Bid Time and Nature gently spare
>   The shaft we raise to them and thee.

A PILGRIM IN CONCORD

Rura quae Liris quietâ
Mordet aquâ, taciturnus amnis.

THE Concord School of Philosophy opened its first session in the summer of 1879. The dust of late July lay velvet soft and velvet deep on all the highways; or, stirred by the passing wheel, rose in slow clouds, not unemblematic of the transcendental haze which filled the mental atmosphere thereabout.

Of those who had made Concord one of the homes of the soul, Hawthorne and Thoreau had been dead many years—I saw their graves in Sleepy Hollow;—and Margaret Fuller had perished long ago by shipwreck on Fire Island Beach. But Alcott was still alive and garrulous; and Ellery Channing—Thoreau's biographer— was alive. Above all, the sage of Concord, "the friend and aider of those who would live in the spirit," still walked his ancient haunts; his mind in many ways yet unimpaired, though sadly troubled by aphasia, or the failure of verbal memory. It was an instance of pathetic irony that in his lecture on

59

"Memory," delivered in the Town Hall, he was prompted constantly by his daughter.

It seemed an inappropriate manner of arrival—the Fitchburg Railroad. One should have dropped down upon the sacred spot by parachute; or, at worst, have come on foot, with staff and scrip, along the Lexington pike, reversing the fleeing steps of the British regulars on that April day, when the embattled farmers made their famous stand. But I remembered that Thoreau, whose Walden solitude was disturbed by gangs of Irish laborers laying the tracks of this same Fitchburg Railroad, consoled himself with the reflection that hospitable nature made the intruder a part of herself. The embankment runs along one end of the pond, and the hermit only said:

> It fills a few hollows
> And makes banks for the swallows,
> And sets the sand a-blowing
> And the black-berries growing.

Afterwards I witnessed, and participated in, a more radical profanation of these crystal waters, when two hundred of the dirtiest children in Boston, South-enders, were brought down by train on a fresh-air-fund picnic and washed in the lake just in front of the spot where Thoreau's cabin stood, after having been duly swung in the swings,

teetered on the see-saws, and fed with a sand-
wich, a slice of cake, a pint of peanuts, and
a lemonade apiece, by a committee of chari-
table ladies—one of whom was Miss Louisa
Alcott, certainly a high authority on "Little
Women" and "Little Men."

Miss Alcott I had encountered on the
evening of my first day in Concord, when I
rang the door bell of the Alcott residence
and asked if the seer was within. I fancied
that there was a trace of acerbity in the
manner of the tall lady who answered my
ring, and told me abruptly that Mr. Alcott
was not at home, and that I would probably
find him at Mr. Sanborn's farther up the
street. Perspiring philosophers with dust-
ers and grip-sacks had been arriving all day
and applying at the Alcott house for addresses of boarding houses and for instruc-
tions of all kinds; and Miss Louisa's patience
may well have been tried. She did not take
much stock in the School anyway. Her
father was supremely happy. One of the
dreams of his life was realized, and endless
talk and soul-communion were in prospect.
But his daughter's view of philosophy was
tinged with irony, as was not unnatural in
a high-spirited woman who had borne the
burden of the family's support, and had even
worked out in domestic service, while her un-
worldly parent was transcendentalizing about

the country, holding conversation classes in western towns, from which after prolonged absences he sometimes brought home a dollar, and sometimes only himself. "Philosophy can bake no bread, but it can give us God, freedom, and immortality" read the motto— from Novalis—on the cover of the *Journal of Speculative Philosophy*, published at Concord in those years, under the editorship of Mr. William T. Harris; but bread must be baked, for even philosophers must eat, and an occasional impatience of the merely ideal may be forgiven in the overworked practician.

On Mr. Frank Sanborn's wide, shady verandah, I found Mr. Alcott, a most quaint and venerable figure, large in frame and countenance, with beautiful, flowing white hair. He moved slowly, and spoke deliberately in a rich voice. His face had a look of mild and innocent solemnity, and he reminded me altogether of a large benignant sheep or other ruminating animal. He was benevolently interested when I introduced myself as the first fruits of the stranger and added that I was from Connecticut. He himself was a native of the little hill town of Wolcott, not many miles from New Haven, and in youth had travelled through the South as a Yankee peddler. "Connecticut gave him birth," says Thoreau; "he peddled first her wares, afterwards, he declares, his brains."

A PILGRIM IN CONCORD

Mr. Sanborn was the secretary of the School, and with him I enrolled myself as a pupil and paid the very modest fee which admitted me to its symposia. Mr. Sanborn is well known through his contributions to Concord history and biography. He was for years one of the literary staff of *The Springfield Republican*, active in many reform movements, and an efficient member of the American Social Science Association. Almost from his house John Brown started on his Harper's Ferry raid, and people in Concord still dwell upon the exciting incident of Mr. Sanborn's arrest in 1860 as an accessory before the fact. The United States deputy marshal with his myrmidons drove out from Boston in a hack. They lured the unsuspecting abolitionist outside his door, on some pretext or other, clapped the handcuffs on him, and tried to get him into the hack. But their victim, planting his long legs one on each side of the carriage door, resisted sturdily, and his neighbors assaulted the officers with hue and cry. The town rose upon them. Judge Hoar hastily issued a habeas corpus returnable before the Massachusetts Supreme Court, and the baffled minions of the slave power went back to Boston.

The School assembled in the Orchard House, formerly the residence of Mr. Alcott, on the Lexington road. Next door was the Wayside, Hawthorne's home for a number of years, a cottage overshadowed by the steep hillside that rose behind it, thick with hemlocks and larches. On the ridge of this hill was Hawthorne's "out door study," a foot path worn by his own feet, as he paced back and forth among the trees and thought out the plots of his romances. In 1879 the Wayside was tenanted by George Lathrop, who had married Hawthorne's daughter, Rose. He had already published his "Study of Hawthorne" and a volume of poems, "Rose and Rooftree." His novel, "An Echo of Passion," was yet to come, a book which unites something of modern realism with a delicately symbolic art akin to Hawthorne's own.

A bust of Plato presided over the exercises of the School, and "Plato-Skimpole"— as Mr. Alcott was once nicknamed—made the opening address. I remember how impressively he quoted Milton's lines:

How charming is divine philosophy!
Not harsh and crabbed, as dull fools suppose,
But musical as is Apollo's lute.

Our *pièce de résistance* was the course of lectures in which Mr. Harris expounded Hegel. But there were many other lecturers. Mrs. Edna Cheney talked to us about art;

though all that I recall of her conversation is the fact that she pronounced *always* *olways*, and I wondered if that was the regular Boston pronunciation. Dr. Jones, the self-taught Platonist of Jacksonville, Illinois, interpreted Plato. Quite a throng of his disciples, mostly women, had followed him from Illinois and swelled the numbers of the Summer School. Once Professor Benjamin Peirce, the great Harvard mathematician, came over from Cambridge, and read us one of his Lowell Institute lectures, on the Ideality of Mathematics. He had a most distinguished presence and an eye, as was said, of black fire. The Harvard undergraduates of my time used to call him Benny Peirce; and on the fly leaves of their mathematical text books they would write, "Who steals my Peirce steals trash." Colonel T. W. Higginson read a single lecture on American literature, from which I carried away for future use a delightful story about an excellent Boston merchant who, being asked at a Goethe birthday dinner to make a few remarks, said that he "guessed that Go-ethe was the N. P. Willis of Germany."

Colonel Higginson's lecture was to me a green oasis in the arid desert of metaphysics, but it was regarded by earnest truth-seekers in the class as quite irrelevant to the purposes of the course. The lecturer himself confided

to me at the close of the session a suspicion
that his audience cared more for philosophy
than for literature. Once or twice Mr.
Emerson visited the School, taking no part
in its proceedings, but sitting patiently
through the hour, and wearing what a newspaper reporter described as his "wise smile."
After the lecture for the session was ended,
the subject was thrown open to discussion
and there was an opportunity to ask questions. Most of us were shy to speak out in
that presence, feeling ourselves in a state of
pupilage. Usually there would be a silence
of several minutes, as at a Quaker meeting
waiting for the spirit to move; and then Mr.
Alcott would announce in his solemn, musical
tones "I have a thought"; and after a
weighty pause, proceed to some Orphic utter-
ance. Alcott, indeed, was what might be
called the leader on the floor; and he was
ably seconded by Miss Elizabeth Peabody,
the sister of Nathaniel Hawthorne's wife.
Miss Peabody was well known as the intro-
ducer of the German kindergarten, and for
her life-long zeal in behalf of all kinds of
philanthropies and reforms. Henry James
was accused of having caricatured her in his
novel "The Bostonians," in the figure of the
dear, visionary, vaguely benevolent old lady
who is perpetually engaged in promoting
"causes," attending conventions, carrying

on correspondence, forming committees, drawing up resolutions, and the like; and who has so many "causes" on hand at once that she gets them all mixed up and cannot remember which of her friends are spiritualists and which of them are concerned in woman's rights movements, temperance agitations, and universal peace associations. Mr. James denied that he meant Miss Peabody, whom he had never met or known. If so, he certainly divined the type. In her later years, Miss Peabody was nicknamed "the grandmother of Boston."

I have to acknowledge, to my shame, that I was often a truant to the discussions of the School, which met three hours in the morning and three in the afternoon. The weather was hot and the air in the Orchard House was drowsy. There were many outside attractions, and more and more I was tempted to leave the philosophers to reason high—

Of providence, foreknowledge, will, and fate—
Fixed fate, free will, foreknowledge absolute—

while I wandered off through the woods for a bath in Walden, some one and a half miles away, through whose transparent waters the pebbles on the bottom could be plainly seen at a depth of thirty feet. Sometimes I went farther afield to White Pond, described by

Thoreau, or Baker Farm, sung by Ellery
Channing. A pleasant young fellow at Miss
Emma Barrett's boarding house, who had
no philosophy, but was a great hand at
picnics and boating and black-berrying
parties, paddled me up the Assabeth, or
North Branch, in his canoe, and drove me
over to Longfellow's Wayside Inn at Sudbury. And so it happens that, when I look
back at my fortnight at Concord, what I
think of is not so much the murmurous
auditorium of the Orchard House, as the row
of colossal sycamores along the village sidewalk that led us thither, whose smooth,
mottled trunks in the moonlight resembled a
range of Egyptian temple columns. Or I
haunt again at twilight the grounds of the
Old Manse, where Hawthorne wrote his
"Mosses," and the grassy lane beside it lead-
ing down to the site of the rude bridge and
the first battlefield of the Revolution. Here
were the headstones of the two British soldiers, buried where they fell; here the Concord monument erected in 1836:

> On this green bank, by this soft stream
>   We set to-day a votive stone:
> That memory may their deed redeem
>   When, like our sires, our sons are gone.

In the field across the river was the spirited
statue of the minuteman, designed by young

Daniel Chester French, a Concord boy who has since distinguished himself as a sculptor in wider fields and more imposing works.

The social life of Concord, judging from such glimpses as could be had of it, was peculiar. It was the life of a village community, marked by the friendly simplicity of country neighbors, but marked also by unusual intellectual distinction and an addiction to "the things of the mind." The town was not at all provincial, or what the Germans call *kleinstädtisch:*—cosmopolitan, rather, as lying on the highway of thought. It gave one a thrill, for example, to meet Mr. Emerson coming from the Post Office with his mail, like any ordinary citizen. The petty constraint, the narrow standards of conduct which are sometimes the bane of village life were almost unknown. Transcendental freedom of speculation, all manner of heterodoxies, and the individual queernesses of those whom the world calls "cranks," had produced a general tolerance. Thus it was said, that the only reason why services were held in the Unitarian Church on Sunday was because Judge Hoar didn't quite like to play whist on that day. Many of the Concord houses have gardens bordering upon the river; and I was interested to notice that the boats moored at the bank had painted on their sterns plant names or bird names

taken from the Concord poems—such as
"The Rhodora," "The Veery," "The Lin-
næa," and "The Wood Thrush." Many a
summer hour I spent with Edward Hoar in
his skiff, rowing, or sailing, or floating up
and down on this soft Concord stream—
Musketaquit, or "grass-ground river"—
moving through miles of meadow, fringed
with willows and button bushes, with a cur-
rent so languid, said Hawthorne, that the
eye cannot detect which way it flows. Sometimes we sailed as far as Fair Haven Bay,
whose "dark and sober billows," "when the
wind blows freshly on a raw March day,"
Thoreau thought as fine as anything on Lake
Huron or the northwest coast. Nor were we,
I hope, altogether unperceiving of that other
river which Emerson detected flowing under-
neath the Concord—

Thy summer voice, Musketaquit,
  Repeats the music of the rain,
But sweeter rivers pulsing flit
  Through thee as though through Concord
      plain. . . .

I see the inundation sweet,
  I hear the spending of the stream,
Through years, through men, through nature
      fleet,
  Through love and thought, through power
      and dream.

Edward Hoar had been Thoreau's companion in one of his visits to the Maine woods. He knew the flora and fauna of Concord as well as his friend the poet-naturalist. He had a large experience of the world, had run a ranch in New Mexico and an orange plantation in Sicily. He was not so well known to the public as his brothers, Rockwood Hoar, Attorney General in Grant's Cabinet, and the late Senator George Frisbie Hoar, of Worcester; but I am persuaded that he was just as good company; and, then, neither of these distinguished gentlemen would have wasted whole afternoons in eating the lotus along the quiet reaches of the Musketaquit with a stripling philosopher.

The appetite for discussion not being fully satisfied by the stated meetings of the School in the Orchard House, the hospitable Concord folks opened their houses for informal symposia in the evenings. I was privileged to make one of a company that gathered in Emerson's library. The subject for the evening was Shakespeare, and Emerson read, by request, that mysterious little poem "The Phœnix and the Turtle," attributed to Shakespeare on rather doubtful evidence, but included for some reason in Emerson's volume of favorite selections, "Parnassus." He began by saying that he would not himself have chosen this particular piece, but as

it had been chosen for him he would read it.
And this he did, with that clean-cut, refined
enunciation and subtle distribution of em-
phasis which made the charm of his delivery
as a lyceum lecturer. When he came to the
couplet,

> Truth may seem, but cannot be,
> Beauty brag, but 'tis not she,

I thought that I detected an idealistic impli-
cation in the lines which accounted for their
presence in "Parnassus."

That shy recluse, Ellery Channing, most
eccentric of the transcendentalists, was not
to be found at the School or the evening
symposia. He had married a sister of Margaret Fuller, but for years he had lived alone
and done for himself, and his oddities had
increased upon him with the years. I had
read and liked many of his poems—those
poems so savagely cut up by Poe, when first
published in 1843—and my expressed interest in these foundlings of the Muse gave
me the opportunity to meet the author of
"A Poet's Hope" at one hospitable table
where he was accustomed to sup on a stated
evening every week.

The Concord Summer School of Philosophy went on for ten successive years, but I
never managed to attend another session.
A friend from New Haven, who was there

for a few days in 1880, brought back the news that a certain young lady who was just beginning the study of Hegel the year before, had now got up to the second intention, and hoped in time to attain the sixth. I never got far enough in Mr. Harris's lectures to discover what Hegelian intentions were; but my friend spoke of them as if they were something like degrees in Masonry. In 1905 I visited Concord for the first and only time in twenty-six years. There is a good deal of philosophy in Wordsworth's Yarrow poems—

> For when we're there, although 'tis fair,
> 'Twill be another Yarrow!—

and I have heard it suggested that he might well have added to his trilogy, a fourth member, "Yarrow Unrevisited." There is a loss, though Concord bears the strain better than most places, I think. As we go on in life the world gets full of ghosts, and at the capital of transcendentalism I was peculiarly conscious of the haunting of these spiritual presences. Since I had been there before, Emerson and Alcott and Ellery Channing and my courteous host and companion, Edward Hoar, and my kind old landlady Miss Barrett—who had also been Emerson's landlady and indeed everybody's landlady in Concord, and whom her youngest boarders

addressed affectionately as Emma—all these
and many more had joined the sleepers in
Sleepy Hollow. The town itself has suffered
comparatively few changes. True there is
a trolley line through the main street—oddly
called "The Milldam," and in Walden wood
I met an automobile not far from the cairn,
or stone pile, which marks the site of Thoreau's cabin. But the woods themselves were
intact and the limpid waters of the pond had
not been tapped to furnish power for any
electric light company. The Old Manse
looked much the same, and so did the Wayside and the Orchard House. Not a tree was
missing from the mystic ring of tall pines
in front of Emerson's house at the fork of
the Cambridge and Lexington roads. On
the central square the ancient tavern was
gone where I had lodged on the night of my
arrival and where my host, a practical philosopher—everyone in Concord had his philosophy,—took a gloomy view of the local
potentialities of the hotel business. He said
there was nothing doing—some milk and
asparagus were raised for the Boston market,
but the inhabitants were mostly literary
people. "I suppose," he added, "we've got
the smartest literary man in the country
living right here." "You mean Mr. Emerson," I suggested. "Yes, sir, and a gentleman too."

"And Alcott?" I ventured.

"Oh, Alcott! The best thing he ever did was his daughters."

This inn was gone, but the still more ancient one across the square remains, the tavern where Major Pitcairn dined on the day of the Lexington fight, and from whose windows or door steps he is alleged by the history books to have cried to a group of embattled farmers, "Disperse, ye Yankee rebels."

Concord is well preserved. Still there are subtle indications of the flight of time. For one thing, the literary pilgrimage business has increased, partly no doubt because trolleys, automobiles, and bicycles have made the town more accessible; but also because our literature is a generation older than it was in 1879. The study of American authors has been systematically introduced into the public schools. The men who made Concord famous are dead, but their habitat has become increasingly classic ground as they themselves have receded into a dignified, historic past. At any rate, the trail of the excursionist—the "cheap tripper," as he is called in England,—is over it all. Basket parties had evidently eaten many a luncheon on the first battle-field of the Revolution, and notices were posted about, asking the public not to deface the trees, and instructing them where to put their paper wrappers and *fragmenta regalia*. I could imagine Boston schoolma'ams pointing out to their classes, the minuteman, the monument, and other objects of interest, and calling for names and dates. The shores of Walden were trampled and worn in spots. There were springboards there for diving, and traces of the picnicker were everywhere. Trespassers were warned away from the grounds of the Old Manse and similar historic spots, by signs of "Private Property."

Concord has grown more self-conscious under the pressure of all this publicity and resort. Tablets and inscriptions have been put up at points of interest. As I was reading one of these on the square, I was approached by a man who handed me a business card with photographs of the monument, the Wayside, the four-hundred-year-old oak, with information to the effect that Mr. ―― would furnish guides and livery teams about the town and to places as far distant as Walden Pond and Sudbury Inn. Thus poetry becomes an asset, and transcendentalism is exploited after the poet and the philosopher are dead. It took Emerson eleven years to sell five hundred copies of "Nature," and Thoreau's books came back upon his hands as unsalable and were piled up in the attic like cord-wood. I was impressed anew with the tameness of the Concord landscape. There is nothing salient about it: it is the average mean of New England nature. Berkshire is incomparably more beautiful. And yet those flat meadows and low hills and slow streams are dear to the imagination, since genius has looked upon them and made them its own. "The eye," said Emerson, "is the first circle: the horizon the second."

And the Concord books—how do they bear the test of revisitation? To me, at least, they have—even some of the second-rate papers in the "Dial" have—now nearly fifty years since I read them first, that freshness which is the mark of immortality.

> No ray is dimmed, no atom worn:
>   My oldest force is good as new;
> And the fresh rose on yonder thorn
>   Gives back the bending heavens in dew.

I think I do not mistake, and confer upon them the youth which was then mine. No, the morning light had touched their foreheads: the youthfulness was in *them*.

Lately I saw a newspaper item about one of the thirty thousand literary pilgrims who are said to visit Concord annually. Calling upon Mr. Sanborn, he asked him which of the Concord authors he thought would last longest. The answer, somewhat to his surprise, was "Thoreau." I do not know whether this report is authentic; but supposing it true, it is not inexplicable. I will confess that, of recent years, I find myself reading Thoreau more and Emerson less. "Walden" seems to me more of a book than Emerson ever wrote. Emerson's was incomparably the larger nature, the more liberal and gracious soul. His, too, was the seminal mind; though Lowell was unfair to the disciple, when he described him as a pistillate blossom fertilized by the Emersonian pollen. For Thoreau had an originality of his own—a flavor as individual as the tang of the bog cranberry, or the wild apples which he loved. One secure advantage he possesses in the concreteness of his subject-matter. The master, with his abstract habit of mind and his view of the merely phenomenal character of the objects of sense, took up a somewhat incurious attitude towards details, not thinking it worth while to "examine too microscopically the universal tablet." The disciple, though he professed that the other world was all his art, had a sharp eye for this. Emerson was Nature's lover, but Thoreau was her scholar. Emerson's method was intuition, while Thoreau's was observation. He worked harder than Emerson and knew more,—that is, within certain defined limits. Thus he read the Greek poets in the original.

Emerson, in whom there was a spice of indolence—due, say his biographers, to feeble health in early life, and the need of going slow,—read them in translations and excused himself on the ground that he liked to be beholden to the great English language.

Compare Hawthorne's description, in the "Mosses," of a day spent on the Assabeth with Ellery Channing, with any chapter in Thoreau's "Week." Moonlight and high noon! The great romancer gives a dreamy, poetic version of the river landscape, musically phrased, pictorially composed, dissolved in atmosphere—a lovely piece of literary art, with the soft blur of a mezzotint engraving, say, from the designs by Turner in Rogers's "Italy." Thoreau, equally imaginative in his way, writes like a botanist, naturalist, surveyor, and local antiquary; and in a pungent, practical, business-like style—a style, as was said of Dante, in which words are things. Yet which of these was the true transcendentalist?

Matthew Arnold's discourse on Emerson was received with strong dissent in Boston, where it was delivered, and in Concord, where it was read with indignation. The critic seemed to be taking away, one after another, our venerated master's claims as a poet, a man of letters, and a philosopher. What! Gray a great poet, and Emerson not! Addi-

son a great writer, and Emerson not! Surely
there are heights and depths in Emerson, an
inspiring power, an originality and force of
thought which are neither in Gray nor in
Addison. And how can these denials be con-
sistent with the sentence near the end of the
discourse, pronouncing Emerson's essays
the most important work done in English
prose during the nineteenth century—more
important than Carlyle's? A truly enormous
concession this; how to reconcile it with those
preceding blasphemies?

Let not the lightning strike me if I say
that I think Arnold was right—as he usually
was right in a question of taste or critical
discernment. For Emerson was essentially
a prophet and theosophist, and not a man of
letters, or creative artist. He could not have
written a song or a story or a play. Arnold
complains of his want of concreteness. The
essay was his chosen medium, well-nigh the
least concrete, the least literary of forms.
And it was not even the personal essay, like
Elia's, that he practised, but an abstract
variety, a lyceum lecture, a moralizing discourse or sermon. For the clerical virus was
strong in Emerson, and it was not for nothing that he was descended from eight generations of preachers. His concern was pri-
marily with religion and ethics, not with the
tragedy and comedy of personal lives, this

motley face of things, *das bunte Menschenle-
ben.* Anecdotes and testimonies abound to
illustrate this. See him on his travels in
Europe, least picturesque of tourists, hastening with almost comic precipitation past
galleries, cathedrals, ancient ruins, Swiss
alps, Como lakes, Rhine castles, Venetian
lagoons, costumed peasants, "the great sinful
streets of Naples"—and of Paris,—and all
manner and description of local color and
historic associations; hastening to meet and
talk with "a few minds"—Landor, Wordsworth, Carlyle. Here he was in line, indeed,
with his great friend, impatiently waving
aside the art patter, with which Sterling
filled his letters from Italy. "Among the
windy gospels," complains Carlyle, "addressed to our poor Century there are few
louder than this of Art. . . . It is a subject
on which earnest men . . . had better . . .
'perambulate their picture-gallery with little
or no speech.' " "Emerson has never in his
life," affirms Mr. John Jay Chapman, "felt
the normal appeal of any painting, or any
sculpture, or any architecture, or any music.
These things, of which he does not know the
meaning in real life, he yet uses, and uses
constantly, as symbols to convey ethical
truths. The result is that his books are full
of blind places, like the notes which will not
strike on a sick piano." The biographers

tell us that he had no ear for music and could
not distinguish one tune from another; did
not care for pictures nor for garden flowers;
could see nothing in Dante's poetry nor in
Shelley's, nor in Hawthorne's romances, nor
in the novels of Dickens and Jane Austen.
Edgar Poe was to him "the jingle man."
Poe, of course, had no "message."

I read, a number of years ago, some impressions of Concord by Roger Riordan, the
poet and art critic. I cannot now put my
hand, for purposes of quotation, upon the
title of the periodical in which these ap-
peared; but I remember that the writer was
greatly amused, as well as somewhat pro-
voked, by his inability to get any of the philosophers with whom he sought interviews to
take an æsthetic view of any poem, or painting, or other art product. They would talk
of its "message" or its "ethical content";
but as to questions of technique or beauty,
they gently put them one side as unworthy
to engage the attention of earnest souls.

At the symposium which I have mentioned
in Emerson's library, was present a young
philosopher who had had the advantage of
reading—perhaps in proof sheets—a book
about Shakespeare by Mr. Denton J. Snider.
He was questioned by some of the guests as
to the character of the work, but modestly
declined to essay a description of it in the

presence of such eminent persons; venturing only to say that it "gave the ethical view of Shakespeare," information which was received by the company with silent but manifest approval.

Yet, after all, what does it matter whether Emerson was singly any one of those things which Matthew Arnold says he was not— great poet, great writer, great philosophical thinker? These are matters of classification and definition. We know well enough the rare combination of qualities which made him our Emerson. Let us leave it there. Even as a formal verse-writer, when he does emerge from his cloud of encumbrances, it is in some supernal phrase such as only the great poets have the secret of:

Music pours on mortals its beautiful disdain;

or:

Have I a lover who is noble and free?
I would he were nobler than to love me.

A WORDLET ABOUT WHITMAN

IN this year many fames have come of age;
among them, Lowell's and Walt Whitman's. As we read their centenary tributes,
we are reminded that Lowell never accepted
Whitman, who was piqued by the fact and
referred to it a number of times in the con-
versations reported by the Boswellian Trau-
bel. Whitmanites explain this want of appre-
ciation as owing to Lowell's conventional
literary standards.

Now convention is one of the things that
distinguish man from the inferior animals.
Language is a convention, law is a convention; and so are the church and the state,
morals, manners, clothing—*teste* "Sartor
Resartus." Shame is a convention: it is
human. The animals are without shame, and
so is Whitman. His "Children of Adam" are
the children of our common father before he
had tasted the forbidden fruit and discovered
that he was naked.

Poetry, too, has its conventions, among
them, metre, rhythm, and rhyme, the choice
of certain words, phrases, images, and
topics, and the rejection of certain others.
Lowell was conservative by nature and thor-

oughly steeped in the tradition of letters. Perhaps he was too tightly bound by these fetters of convention to relish their sudden loosening. I wonder what he would have thought of his kinswoman Amy's free verses if he had lived to read them.

If a large, good-natured, clean, healthy animal could write poetry, it would write much such poetry as the "Leaves of Grass." It would tell how good it is to lie and bask in the warm sun; to stand in cool, flowing water, to be naked in the fresh air; to troop with friendly companions and embrace one's mate. "Leaves of Grass" is the poetry of pure sensation, and mainly, though not wholly, of physical sensation. In a famous passage the poet says that he wants to go away and live with the animals. Not one of them is respectable or sorry or conscientious or worried about its sins.

But his poetry, though animal to a degree, is not unhuman. We do not know enough about the psychology of the animals to be sure whether, or not, they have any sense of the world as a whole. Does an elephant or an eagle perhaps, viewing some immense landscape, catch any glimpse of the universe, as an object of contemplation, apart from the satisfaction of his own sensual needs? Probably not. But Whitman, as has been said a hundred times, was "cosmic." He had an unequalled sense of the bigness of creation and of "these States." He owned a panoramic eye and a large passive imagination, and did well to loaf and let the tides of sensation flow over his soul, drawing out what music was in him without much care for arrangement or selection.

I once heard an admirer of Walt challenged to name a single masterpiece of his production. Where was his perfect poem, his gem of flawless workmanship? He answered, in effect, that he didn't make masterpieces. His poetry was diffused, like the grass blades that symbolized for him our democratic masses.

Of course, the man in the street thinks that Walt Whitman's stuff is not poetry at all, but just bad prose. He acknowledges that there are splendid lines, phrases, and whole passages. There is that one beginning, "I open my scuttle at night," and that glorious apostrophe to the summer night, "Night of south winds, night of the large, few stars." But, as a whole, his work is tiresome and without art. It is alive, to be sure, but so is protoplasm. Life is the first thing and form is secondary; yet form, too, is important. The musician, too lazy or too impatient to master his instrument, breaks it, and seizes a megaphone. Shall we call that originality or failure?

It is also a commonplace that the democratic masses of America have never accepted
Walt Whitman as their spokesman. They
do not read him, do not understand or care
for him. They like Longfellow, Whittier,
and James Whitcomb Riley, poets of sentiment and domestic life, truly poets of the
people. No man can be a spokesman for
America who lacks a sense of humor, and
Whitman was utterly devoid of it, took himself most seriously, posed as a prophet. I
do not say that humor is a desirable quality.
The thesis may even be maintained that it is
a disease of the mind, a false way of looking
at things. Many great poets have been
without it—Milton for example. Shelley
used to speak of "the withering and pervert-
ing power of comedy." But Shelley was
slightly mad. At all events, our really
democratic writers have been such as Mark
Twain and James Whitcomb Riley. I do
not know what Mark Twain thought of Walt,
but I know what Riley thought of him. He
thought him a grand humbug. Certainly if
he had had any sense of humor he would not
have peppered his poems so naïvely with foreign words, calling out "Camerado!" ever and
anon, and speaking of a perfectly good
American sidewalk as a "trottoir" *quasi
Lutetia Parisii*. And if he had not had a
streak of humbug in him, he would hardly

have written anonymous puffs of his own poetry.

But I am far from thinking Walt Whitman a humbug. He was a man of genius whose work had a very solid core of genuine meaning. It is good to read him in spots—he is so big and friendly and wholesome; he feels so good, like a man who has just had a cold bath and tingles with the joy of existence.

Whitman was no humbug, but there is surely some humbug about the Whitman *culte*. The Whitmanites deify him. They speak of him constantly as a seer, a man of exalted intellect. I do not believe that he was a great thinker, but only a great feeler. Was he the great poet of America, or even a great poet at all? A great poet includes a great artist, and "Leaves of Grass," as has been pointed out times without number, is the raw material of poetry rather than the finished product.

A friend of mine once wrote an article about Whitman, favorable on the whole, but with qualifications. He got back a copy of it through the mail, with the word "Jackass!" pencilled on the margin by some outraged Whitmaniac. I know what has been said and written in praise of old Walt by critics of high authority, and I go along with them a part of the way, but only a part. And I do not stand in terror of any critics, however authoritative; remembering how even the great Goethe was taken in by Macpherson's "Ossian." A very interesting paper might be written on what illustrious authors have said of each other: what Carlyle said of Newman, for instance; or what Walter Scott said of Joanna Baillie and the like.